NATURAL WONDERS

The Nile River

The Longest River in the World

Erinn Banting

WEIGL PUBLISHERS INC.

Published by Weigl Publishers Inc.
350 5th Avenue, Suite 3304, PMB 6G
New York, NY 10118-0069
USA

Web site: www.weigl.com

Library of Congress Cataloging-in-Publication Data

Banting, Erinn.
  The Nile River / by Erinn Banting.
    p. cm. — (Natural wonders)
  Includes index.
  ISBN 1-59036-269-1 (library binding : alk. paper) 1-59036-275-6 (pbk.)
  1. Nile River—Juvenile literature. I. Title. II. Natural wonders (Weigl Publishers)
  DT117.B166 2004
  916.2—dc22
                                    2004013603
Printed in the United States of America
1 2 3 4 5 6 7 8 9 0   08 07 06 05 04

Editorial Services
BookMark Publishing, Inc.

Editor
Heather C. Hudak

Design
Terry Paulhus

Layout
Biner Design

Photo Researcher
Dawn Friedman,
BookMark Publishing, Inc.

Photo Description
Cover: The Blue Nile Falls in Ethiopia interrupts the smooth course of the Nile River.
Title page: Papyrus plants line the shores of the Nile River.

Contents

The River of Life

The Nile River in Africa has supplied precious water to human civilizations for thousands of years. Water is an important issue in northern Africa since very dry land covers most of the region. In fact, the Nile River cuts right through the largest desert in the world, the Sahara. Along the banks of the Nile, however, life is possible.

The Nile brings drinking water to people. It allows farmers to raise crops. People fish in the Nile's waters. The river provides a transportation channel so people can travel on boats. Thousands of years ago, Ancient Egyptians used the same river for identical reasons. Not surprisingly, people often refer to the Nile as "the River of Life."

▬ **The Nile runs through desert, but along the riverbanks, trees, farms, and civilization thrive.**

Nile River Facts

- The Nile River is 4,160 miles (6,695 kilometers) long. This makes it the longest river in the world.

- The Nile River is unusual because it begins in the south and flows north. Most rivers flow north to south.

- The largest city along the Nile is Cairo, Egypt. It has the largest population of any city in Africa.

- In 1902, the Aswan Dam was the first dam built on the Nile.

Nile River Locator

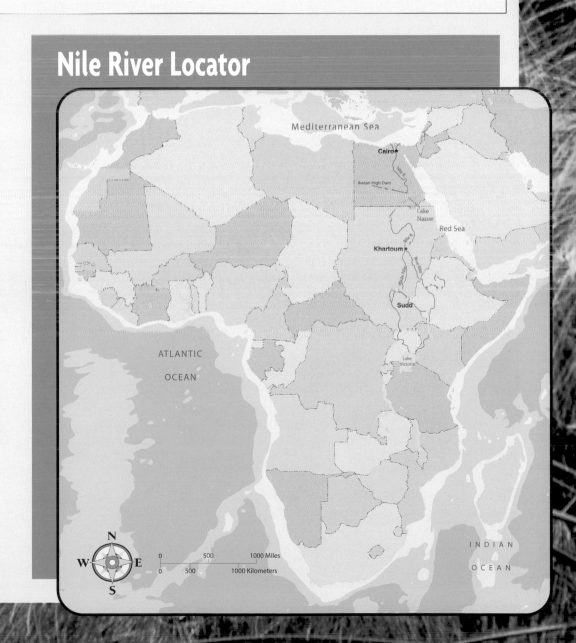

Where in the World?

The Nile River begins as two main branches in central Africa: the White Nile and the Blue Nile. These two branches twist and curve, and generally flow north to Khartoum, Sudan. There, the Blue and White Nile rivers meet, forming the main Nile River. The river then flows up through northeastern Africa until it empties into the Mediterranean Sea.

On its long and winding course, the Nile passes through different environments and various sites. There are swamplands and farmlands, large cities and tiny villages. Pyramids, temples, and other ancient treasures overlook the Nile riverbanks. There is even a huge lake created by humans. All of these and other fascinating sites await a Nile explorer.

▬ Several rocky waterfalls called cataracts interrupt the course of the Nile.

Puzzler

The Nile River, including the Blue and White Nile, twists its way from central Africa up to the northern tip of the continent. In all, the river crosses the borders of nine countries.

Q Can you identify the countries through which the Nile passes?

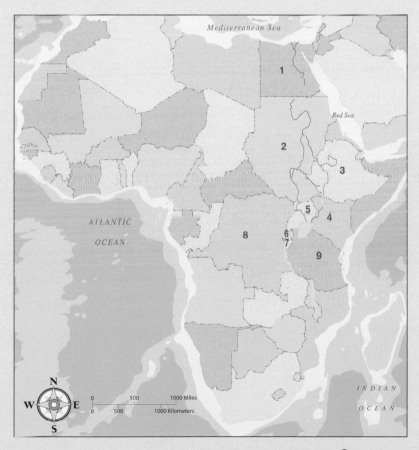

 1. Egypt 2. Sudan 3. Ethiopia 4. Kenya 5. Uganda 6. Rwanda 7. Burundi 8. Democratic Republic of the Congo 9. Tanzania

A Trip Back in Time

Nearly 250 million years ago, Earth's continents split apart from a single, gigantic landmass. Africa then drifted to the place where it rests today. Although Africa stopped drifting, it has never stopped moving. **Geologists** believe that for millions of years, a gradually growing **rift** has been pulling the continent in different directions. The rift is caused by shifting pressure from deep underground.

The rift has already created mountains and valleys on Africa's surface. In some of the valleys, bodies of water have formed. Many of the Nile's sources were formed by the rift, including its major source, Lake Victoria. If the rift continues to grow, geologists believe that larger bodies of water will form. Eventually, an entire ocean could divide the continent. It would take millions of years for this to happen, so people in Africa are not worried.

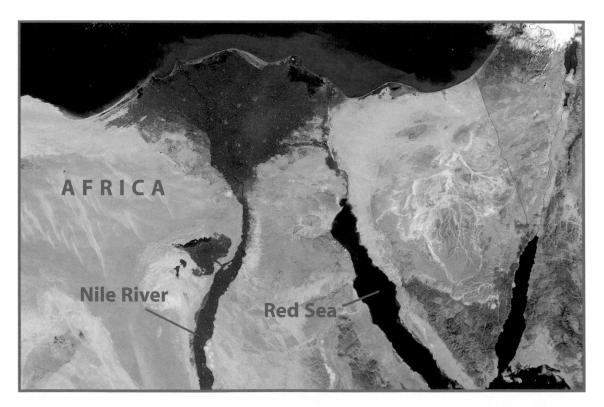

■ **This satellite photo shows how the continental rift has already split land off of Africa by forming the Red Sea.**

Parts of a River

Not every river is the same, but almost all have these main parts, which help to explain how a river works.

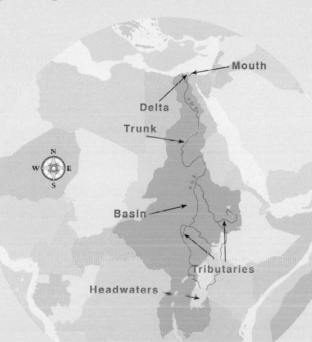

Headwaters: the place where a source of water begins

Tributaries: the large and small rivers and streams that feed water into the main river

Basin: the surrounding land drained by the river and its tributaries

Trunk: the main channel, or "trunk stream," of the river

Delta: the land created by **sediment** the river leaves behind on as it travels to sea

Mouth: the place where the river ends and travels to sea

Water at Work

Water is a necessary resource to every person on Earth, but water can be hard to obtain in the Nile region. Surrounded by desert, Nile River communities would vanish if the Nile were to run dry.

Earth recycles its water. This means that, today, people along the Nile might be using the same water that Ancient Egyptians did. The water cycle describes the way water moves above, on, and below ground. The cycle has four stages.

Storage
Water is stored in oceans, lakes, rivers, and underground. In cold climates, water is also stored in frozen glaciers and icecaps.

Evaporation
When water evaporates, it changes from a liquid to a gas, or vapor. Heat from the Sun speeds up evaporation.

Precipitation
Water vapor collects in clouds. It then falls to the ground as precipitation, such as rain or snow. Every day, precipitation is falling somewhere in the world.

Runoff
Runoff is precipitation that flows into rivers and streams. Runoff water flows above or below ground. Floods occur when too much runoff forces bodies of water to rise over their banks.

The Nile's Water Cycle

The Nile River is part of the water cycle. Using the information provided about the stages of the water cycle, it is easy to understand how the Nile functions.

The Nile is a river, so it stores water. Water also evaporates from the Nile. In one part of the Blue Nile, the water flows into a massive swamp called the Sudd. In this shallow, hot area, water moves much more slowly than in other parts of the river. About half of the Sudd waters are lost to evaporation.

The illustration below shows how the Nile River is involved in the water cycle.

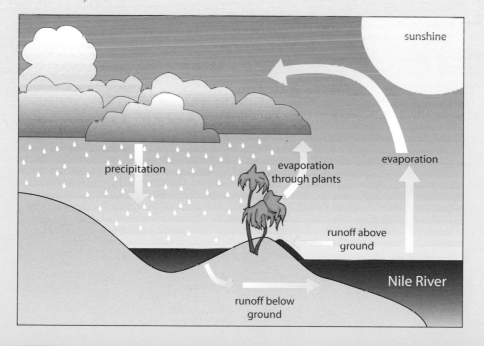

Life Along the River

Hundreds of **species** of plants and animals make their homes in the Nile and along its banks. One of the most common plants found on the Nile shores is papyrus. This long reed has been used by people for thousands of years to make all sorts of objects, such as baskets, roofs for homes, and boats.

Giant Nile perch swim in the waters of the river. These fish grow to be 6 feet (1.8 meters) long. Crocodiles and hippopotamuses also live in the water, coming ashore to bask in the Sun. Bird life along the Nile is varied and vibrant. Beautiful flocks of white egrets hunt the shores for insects and frogs to eat. Swallows, ducks, warblers, and other bird types also live along the Nile. The hoopoe is a bird that lives near the Nile. This bird is rarely seen outside of this area.

■ **Farmers have harvested papyrus along the Nile for centuries. Ancient Egyptians used papyrus to make one of the earliest types of paper.**

Lake Nasser

In 1971, the Aswan High Dam was completed. The dam created a huge lake called Lake Nasser to hold floodwaters. Certain animals have benefited from the new lake, as they have an **ecosystem** in which they can thrive. Fish, birds, mammals, and reptiles now have a home where there was once only rock and sand.

■ **Before the creation of Lake Nasser, the Nile crocodile population was decreasing. Today, these crocodiles are finding new life at the lake and along the river.**

Early Explorers

The great civilizations of Ancient Egypt were built on the shores of the Nile about 5,000 years ago. Today, people are amazed by the huge pyramids and temples the Egyptians built without the aid of heavy machines. For centuries, Ancient Egyptians and many other civilizations were not able to solve one mystery of the Nile. They could not determine the source of the river.

Many explorers attempted to travel the entire course of the Nile to discover its source. It was not until recent centuries when a few determined explorers solved the puzzle, piece by piece. In 1770, Scottish explorer James Bruce found Lake Tana and the river now known as the Blue Nile while traveling overland in Africa. He sailed the river. When it joined with the main Nile, he knew he had discovered a Nile source, Lake Tana. Nearly a century later, in 1862, a British explorer named John Hanning Speke made another discovery. He was the first to learn that Lake Victoria is the source of the White Nile. Unfortunately, Europeans did not believe Speke's claim until other explorers proved him correct years later.

■ Today, people agree that Lake Victoria is the main source of the Nile, and that John Speke was correct, after all.

Biography

Stanley and Livingstone

The exploration of the Nile inspired one of the best-known questions in history: "Dr. Livingstone, I presume?" Dr. David Livingstone was a British explorer who traveled extensively in Africa. In the mid-1800s, Africa was still a mysterious continent to Europeans. Livingstone did more than any other person to uncover Africa's mysteries. On his third and final African adventure, Livingstone's goal was to prove whether or not Lake Victoria was the source of the Nile. He departed in 1866 and was not heard from for several years. In 1869, an American newspaper sent another explorer, Henry Stanley, into Africa to find Livingstone. On November 10, 1871, Stanley found him in an African village surrounded by indigenous people. When they first met face to face, Stanley uttered his famous question.

Stanley and Livingstone continued exploring together briefly. Stanley left Africa to report Livingstone's story to the world. Dr. Livingstone became ill and died in Africa in 1873. Stanley, however, returned to Africa for years of further exploration. In 1875, he made a careful survey of Lake Victoria and finally proved that it was, indeed, the source of the Nile.

Facts of Life

Dr. David Livingstone
Born: 1813
Hometown: Blantyre, Scotland
Occupation: missionary, explorer, and doctor
Died: 1873

Sir Henry Morton Stanley
Born: 1841
Hometown: Denbigh, Wales
Occupation: journalist and explorer
Died: 1904

The Big Picture

Rivers can be found on every continent on Earth, from frozen Antarctica to blazing hot Africa. This map shows the location of a major river in each continent.

ARCTIC OCEAN

NORTH AMERICA

Mississippi River

ATLANTIC OCEAN

PACIFIC OCEAN

Amazon River

SOUTH AMERICA

Map Legend		
North America	Mississippi River	2,340 miles (3,766 km)
South America	Amazon River	4,000 miles (6,437 km)
Europe	Volga River	2,300 (3,701 km)
Asia	Yangtze (Chang) River	3,900 miles (6,276 km)
Africa	Nile River	4,160 miles (6,695 km)
Australia	Murray River	1,609 miles (2,589 km)
Antarctica (not shown)	Onyx River	12 miles (19 km)

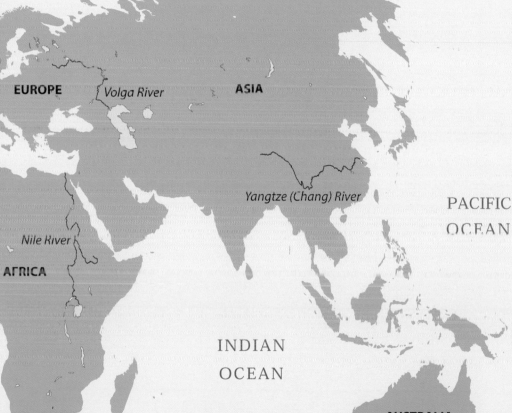

ARCTIC OCEAN

EUROPE   *Volga River*   ASIA

Yangtze (Chang) River

PACIFIC OCEAN

Nile River

AFRICA

INDIAN OCEAN

AUSTRALIA

Murray River

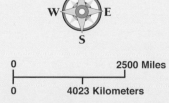

N
W E
S

0   2500 Miles

0   4023 Kilometers

People of the River

The Nile is no longer just the site of an ancient civilization. Today, the Nile River basin is home to about 160 million people. Cairo, Egypt, is a city bursting at its seams with more than 9 million people. The streets are busy with traffic, and tall, modern buildings fill the skyline. People work in office buildings, factories, universities, and other places. People from the very rich to the very poor live in this place, making Cairo very much a modern city of the world.

Along the Nile, however, not all communities are prosperous. For instance, Ethiopia is a world far different from Cairo. Most people near this part of the Blue Nile are rural farmers who never come close to city life. Their lives are difficult. In recent decades, **droughts** and civil war have led to **famine**. Millions of innocent people have died. Charitable organizations work hard to raise money and provide medical care and food to people in Ethiopia, Uganda, and other central African nations.

■ **Cairo straddles the Nile River. Large buildings of the city center are on the east side of the river, and suburbs are on the west side.**

Old and Modern

Imagine living in a place where there are reminders of ancient history just about everywhere you turn. Every day along the Nile, residents live alongside examples of the distant past. The 3,000-year-old Luxor Temple is located in the middle of the modern city of Luxor. People can visit this amazing **artifact** in the course of running daily errands. In Cairo, ancient royal palaces have been turned into modern hotels.

Living in the cradle of ancient history has both good and bad elements. For instance, the tourists who visit these sites spend money that helps the area's economies. The cost of **preserving** these sites, however, is very high. A large portion of the money that tourists spend in the area does not actually help the people. Instead, much of the money is spent on maintaining the ancient artifacts.

■ **A visit to the 4,500-year-old pyramids at Giza is just a half-hour bus ride from Cairo.**

River Stories

Ancient Egyptians believed in many gods and goddesses who ruled different parts of nature. The Nile River was so important that the Egyptians believed it was controlled by a god named Osiris. According to Egyptian mythology, Osiris was a ruler of Egypt who was murdered by his jealous brother, Seth. Osiris's body was cut up, placed in a coffin, and sent floating down the Nile. He eventually came back to life as a god.

The Nile has also inspired more recent authors to write novels, poems, and stories about the river. In the early 1600s, British playwright William Shakespeare wrote a well-known play called *Antony and Cleopatra*. It is based on the real-life story of Cleopatra, an Ancient Egyptian ruler who was nicknamed "the Queen of the Nile." In 1937, author Agatha Christie wrote one of her most well-known mystery novels, *Death on the Nile*, about murder and suspicion aboard a Nile River cruise.

▬ Paintings of Osiris have been discovered on walls of ancient tombs along the Nile.

Ramses II

One of the great stories of the *Bible* is linked to a leader from Egypt's past. Ramses II was **pharaoh** of Egypt from 1290 to 1224 BC. He was well known for building magnificent temples along the Nile River.

Today, however, people may know Ramses more for his role in the biblical story of Moses. According to the *Bible*, Ramses ruled over Jewish slaves in Egypt and refused to release them to freedom. The Jewish people's leader, Moses, engaged Ramses in a battle of wills. Eventually, Ramses freed Moses's people. Today, Jewish people celebrate this story during the Passover holiday.

▬ **The temple of Ramses II stands on the shore of Lake Nasser near the Nile River.**

Natural Attractions

There are many things to see and do on a trip to the Nile River. People tour the river on cruise ships or on traditional boats called *felucca*. In some Nile cities, visitors can step off the boats and walk directly to museums, restaurants, or shopping districts.

Visitors also travel the Nile River to see the river's more natural wonders. The spectacular Tisisat Falls on the Blue Nile draw visitors who travel to Ethiopia. Another popular site is Lake Victoria, the headwaters of the Nile. It is the second-largest freshwater lake in the world. On its islands and shores, visitors can camp, fish, and observe a wondrous array of wildlife.

▬ **Some tour companies offer Nile felucca tours lasting a few hours, several days, or even several weeks.**

Ancient Fruit

From thousands of years ago to today, dates have been one of the favorite foods of Egypt. **Archaeologists** exploring ancient pyramids have found dates placed inside tombs. Presumably, this was so the dead person sealed in the tomb would have something to eat in the afterlife.

Dates grow as the fruit on the date palm tree. After picking the fruit, farmers leave dates in the Sun to dry. They become a sweet, chewy food similar to raisins. Date palms grow well in desert conditions, so dates are a **staple food** in certain parts of northern Africa.

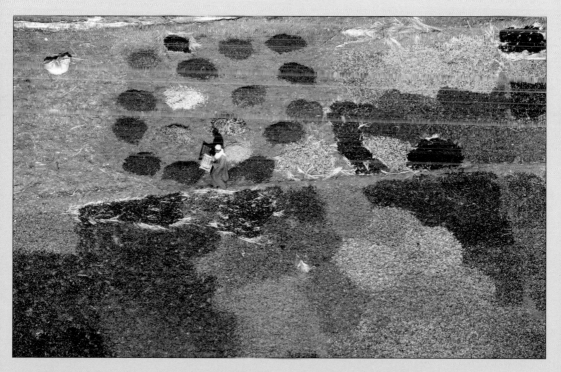

After dates are picked, farmers set them out to dry.

Controlling the River

Since ancient times, people have attempted to control the Nile's floods and make better use of the Nile's water. Over the last century, humans have made major changes to the river. In 1971, the Aswan High Dam was completed. It ended the damaging floods that occurred along the Nile almost every year. The dam includes a power plant that provides electricity to most of Egypt. It also created the huge Lake Nasser **reservoir**.

In addition to blocking water, the dam stops most sediment from traveling up the Nile. This sediment contains important **nutrients** that help create the rich farmland that exists along the river. The entire Nile Delta is land created by thousands of years of sediment pouring from the Nile's mouth.

The Aswan High Dam is more than 2 miles (3.2 km) long.

Today, very little sediment reaches the delta, so the quality of the soil suffers. Some farmers use chemicals to keep their soil healthy. Many scientists believe that foods grown with such chemicals are dangerous to eat. Scientists also believe that the chemicals wash back into the Nile, which can poison its water. So, for all the many benefits a dam can provide, there are quite a few drawbacks as well.

Should humans build dams to control the Nile?	
YES	**NO**
Dams create reservoirs that supply water to people who live nearby. They also run power plants.	Dams stop needed water from reaching places further along the river.
 Dams control seasonal flooding that destroys people's homes along the river.	Annual flooding supplied the river's farms with nutrient-rich soil. Now, the farms do not receive those nutrients. Farmers use chemicals instead.
Dams make it easier to travel by boat on the river by controlling the flow of water.	Dams force people from their homes and destroy historical sites by creating new reservoirs. 

Time Line

The 240-foot- (73-m) long Sphinx resides near the northern Nile banks. The huge stone statue represents a character from Egyptian mythology.

5–4 billion years ago
Earth is formed.

300–200 million years ago
Dinosaurs and mammals begin to develop.

250 million years ago
Earth's continents separate.

65 million years ago
Dinosaurs become extinct.

30 million years ago
The Nile River begins to form.

2–4 million years ago
The first ancestors of humans appear in Africa.

4000–1500 BC
Africa's climate grows drier. The Sahara Desert is formed.

3400 BC
The first great civilization in Ancient Egypt begins.

Elephantine Island may be the oldest settlement on the Nile. Archaeologists have found items there that pre-date the time of the pharaohs.

3100 BC
Kingdoms along the Nile join, forming the Egyptian empire.

1290–1224 BC
Ramses II rules Egypt.

600 BC
Cairo is first settled.

AD 1770
James Bruce reaches the source of the Blue Nile.

Ethiopia's Lake Tana is the main source of the Blue Nile.

In city markets, Nile farmers and fishers sell products they reap from the great river's waters.

1902
The first Aswan Dam is completed. It is the first dam built on the Nile.

1959
A treaty is signed between Egypt and Sudan giving Egypt control of most of the Nile water. The treaty will harm other Nile nations in years to come.

1968
Aswan High Dam begins operating. Its construction is completed in 1971.

1970s–1980s
Civil wars in Sudan and Ethiopia halt development of **irrigation** systems on the Nile.

1980s
Droughts kill millions of Africans. Ethiopia and other Nile areas are hard hit.

1999
The Nile Basin Agreement is formed between the countries through which the Nile passes. This agreement attempts to undo the unfair 1959 treaty.

1864
John Hanning Speke finds that Lake Victoria is the source of the Nile.

1871
Stanley and Livingstone meet in Africa and begin exploring together.

1869
The Suez Canal is completed. The man-made channel links the Mediterranean Sea to the Red Sea.

What Have You Learned?

True or False?

Decide whether the following statements are true or false. If the statement is false, make it true.

1. Papyrus grows along the Nile River.

2. Ramses II was a slave in Egypt.

3. We do not know the source of the Nile River.

4. Dr. David Livingstone explored Africa several different times.

5. Rivers can be found on every continent.

6. The water cycle does not need the Sun.

7. A felucca is a musical instrument.

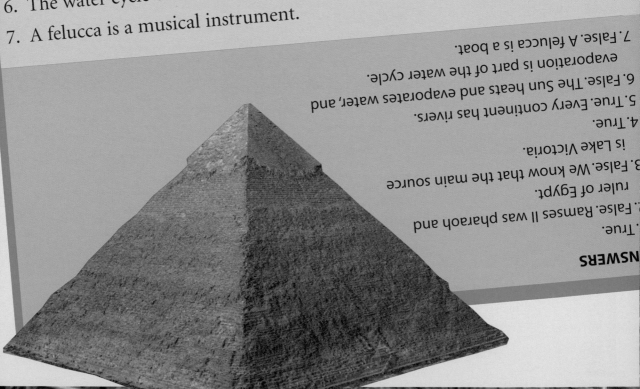

7. False. A felucca is a boat.
6. False. The Sun heats and evaporates water, and evaporation is part of the water cycle.
5. True. Every continent has rivers.
4. True.
3. False. We know that the main source is Lake Victoria.
2. False. Ramses II was pharaoh and ruler of Egypt.
1. True.

ANSWERS

Short Answer

Answer the following questions using information from the book.

1. Is the mouth of the Nile at its beginning or its end?

2. What fruit grows along the Nile?

3. Who wrote *Antony and Cleopatra*?

4. What is the longest river in the United States?

5. Through how many different countries does the Nile River pass?

6. Who was the god of the Nile, according to Egyptian mythology?

ANSWERS
1. the end
2. dates
3. William Shakespeare
4. The Mississippi River
5. Nine
6. Osiris

Multiple Choice

Choose the best answer for the following questions.

1. People along the Nile make paper from:
   a) sediment
   b) papyrus
   c) stone

2. Where do the White Nile and Blue Nile meet?
   a) Khartoum
   b) Cairo
   c) Luxor

3. Which of these countries does not have part of the Nile within its borders?
   a) Rwanda
   b) Egypt
   c) Zimbabwe

4. Which of the following statements is incorrect?
   a) The Nile is the longest river in the world.
   b) Africa might split apart several million years from now.
   c) Lake Nasser existed during the time of Ancient Egypt.

ANSWERS
1. b, 2. a, 3. c, 4. c

Find Out for Yourself

Books

Jackson, Kevin. *Building the Great Pyramid.* Toronto: Firefly Books, 2003.

Millard, Anne. *The Story of the Nile.* London: Dorling Kindersley, 2003.

Parks, Peggy J. *The Aswan High Dam.* San Diego: Blackbirch Press, 2004.

Web Sites

Use the Internet to find out more about the people, plants, animals, and geology of the Nile River and the continent of Africa.

National Geographic: Stanley and Livingstone
www.nationalgeographic.com/features/97/lantern
Learn more about the lives and adventures of Stanley and Livingstone through this Web site.

PBS: Africa
www.pbs.org/wnet/africa
This Web site is a complete, child-friendly tour of the entire continent of Africa.

Wild Egypt
www.touregypt.net/wildegypt
This Web site is an online safari for all ages. Choose a journey down the Nile, over land, or in the Red Sea.

Skill Matching Page

What did you learn? Look at the questions in the "Skills" column. Compare them to the page number of the answers in the "Page" column. Refresh your memory by reading the "Answer" column below.

SKILLS	ANSWER	PAGE
What facts did I learn from this book?	I learned the Nile River is the longest river in the world.	5
What skills did I learn?	I learned how to read maps.	5, 7, 16 17
What activities did I do?	I answered the questions in the quiz.	28–29
How can I find out more?	I can read the books and visit the web sites from the Find Out for Yourself section.	30
How can I get involved?	I can find out how to help African people in need.	18

Glossary

archaeologists: people who dig up objects to learn about ancient civilizations
artifact: an object made by humans; a historical object in a museum
droughts: long periods of dry weather
ecosystem: a group of living plants, animals, and their environment, all of which act as a community
famine: starvation of large numbers of people
geologists: scientists who study rocks, soils, and minerals
irrigation: a way of directing water to land where it is needed
nutrients: any substance that provides nourishment
pharaoh: a king in Ancient Egypt
preserving: saving for the future; shielding from destruction
reservoir: a holding area to store water
rift: a long, narrow crack; a place where land is pulling apart
sediment: material deposited by water, wind, or glaciers
species: a specific group of plant or animal that shares characteristics
staple food: a food that is eaten regularly and is kept in large amounts

Index